American Sign Language

Questions and Answers

by E. Russell Primm III • illustrated by Kathleen Petelinsek

childsworld.com

The Child's World
childsworld.com

Published by The Child's World®
800-599-READ • childsworld.com

Photography Credits
Prostock-studio/Shutterstock.com, cover, 3, 8, 10, 12; PeopleImages.com–Yuri A/Shutterstock.com, 1, 4; Monkey Business Images/Shutterstock.com, 5; Sklo Studio/Shutterstock.com, 6; EZ-Stock Studio/Shutterstock.com, 7; Roquillo Tebar/Shutterstock.com, 9, 17; Krakenimages .com/Shutterstock.com, 11, 20; Q88/Shutterstock.com, 13; Cast Of Thousands/Shutterstock.com, 14; Luis Molinero/Shutterstock.com, 15; karelnoppe/Shutterstock.com, 16; Tienuskin/Shutterstock.com, 18; Sergey Novikov/Shutterstock.com, 19; MIA Studio/Shutterstock.com, 21

ISBN Information
9781503889040 (Reinforced Library Binding)
9781503890121 (Portable Document Format)
9781503891364 (Online Multi-user eBook)
9781503892606 (Electronic Publication)

LCCN 2023950310

BRINGING THE WORLD 19 68 TO YOUNG READERS

Printed in the United States of America

Note to Parents, Caregivers, and Educators: The understanding of any language begins with the acquisition of vocabulary, whether the language is spoken or manual. The books in this series provide readers, both young and old, with basic American Sign Language signs. Combining close photo cues and simple, but detailed, line illustrations, children and adults alike can begin the process of learning American Sign Language.

Let these books be an introduction to the world of American Sign Language. Most languages have regional dialects and multiple ways of expressing the same thought. This is also true for sign language. We have attempted to use the most common version of the signs for the words in this series. As with any language, the best way to learn is to be taught in person by a frequent user. It is our hope that this series will pique your interest in sign language.

A special thanks to our advisers: As a member of a deaf family that spans four generations, **Kim Bianco Majeri** lives, works, and plays among the Deaf community. **Carmine L. Vozzolo** is an educator of children who are deaf and hard of hearing, as well as their families.

E. Russell Primm III was a well-known figure in the publishing industry who produced thousands of acclaimed books for children. He was affiliated with organizations such as the American Library Association, the Chicago Book Clinic, and the University of Chicago Publishing Program Advisory Board.

Kathleen Petelinsek has loved books since she was a child. Through the years, she has written, designed, and illustrated many books for children. She lives in Wisconsin, near her granddaughter who also shares her love for books.

"What?" in Spanish is "¿Qué?" (KAY).

What?

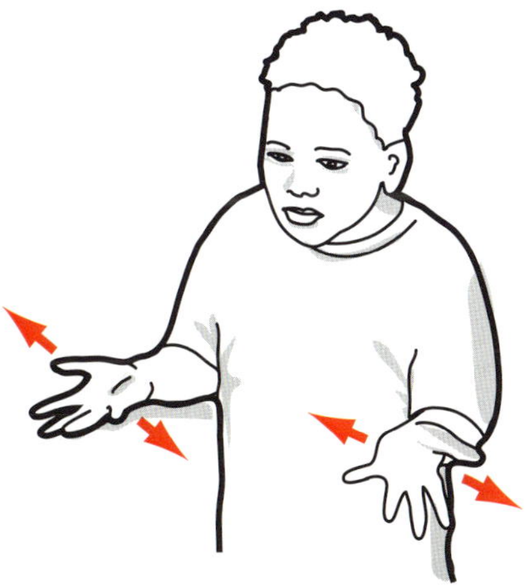

Shrug your shoulders and move your hands slightly from side to side.

"Question" in Spanish is "pregunta" (pray-GOON-tah).

Question

Draw a question mark in the air. (It will look backward to the person you are speaking to.)

"Answer" in German is "antwort" (AHNT-vahrt).

Answer

1.

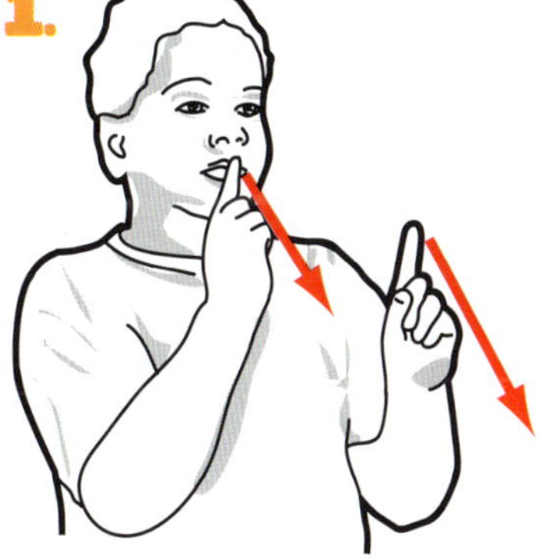

2.

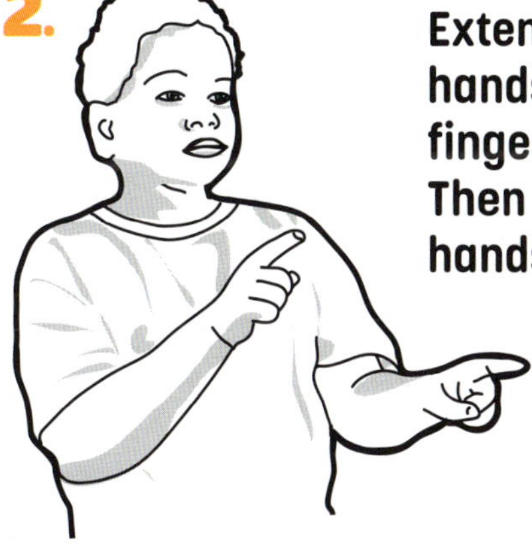

Extend index fingers of both hands. Place your right index finger closer to your mouth. Then swiftly extend both hands outward and down.

"Who?" in Japanese is "Dare?" (DAYR-ay).

Who?

Curl and wiggle your right index finger near your mouth.

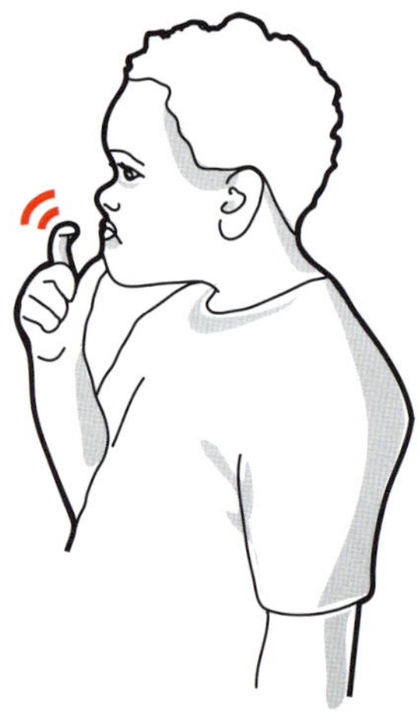

Tapping your watch and shrugging your shoulders can make this sign, too.

When?

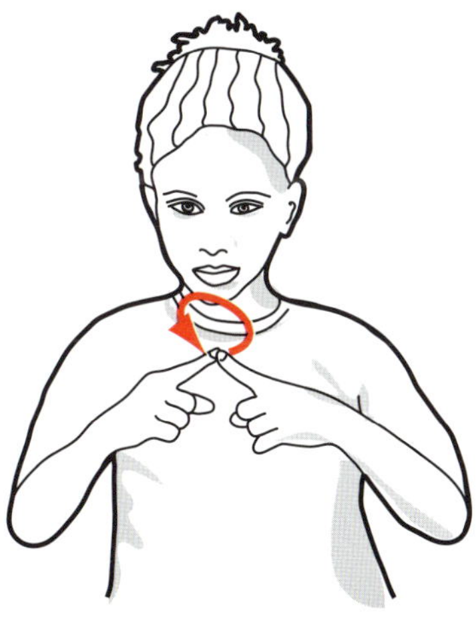

Move your right index finger in a circle around your left index finger.

"Yesterday" in Spanish is "ayer" (ah-YAYR).

Yesterday

Make a fist with your right hand and point your thumb up. Starting with your thumb near your chin, move it up toward your ear.

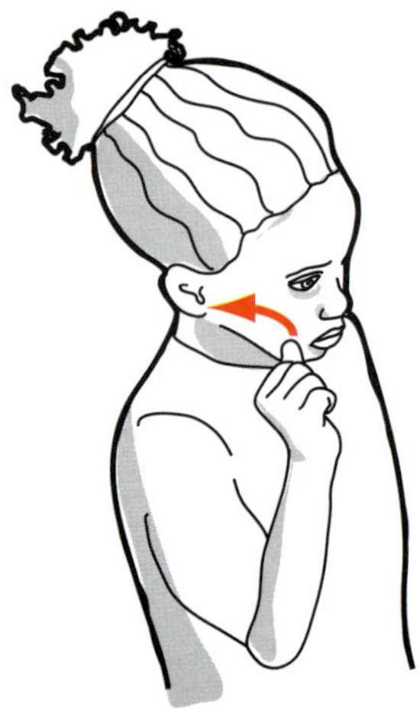

"Today" in German is "heute" (HOY-tuh).

Today

Make the "Y" shape, but face your hands toward you. Motion downward twice.

"Tomorrow" in French is "demain" (deh-MAHN).

Tomorrow

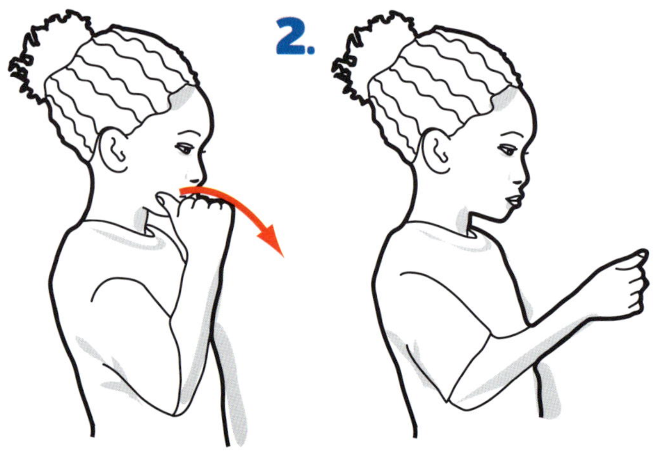

Make a fist with your right hand and point your thumb up. With your hand near your right cheek, move it down and away.

"Where?" in Japanese is "Doko?" (DOH-koh).

Where?

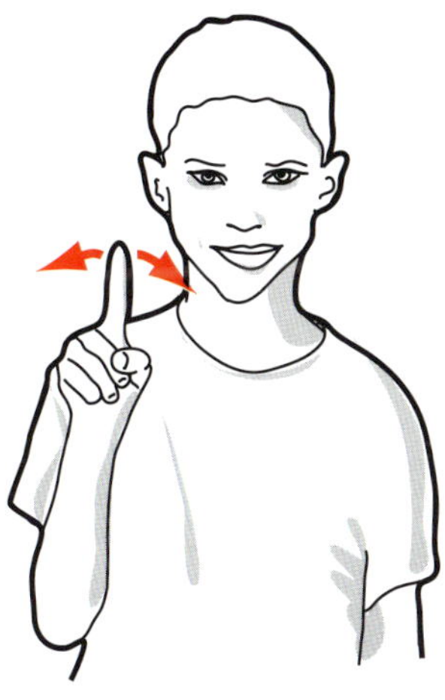

Point your right index finger upward. Then wiggle your wrist slightly from left to right.

"Here" in Spanish is "aquí" (ah-KEE).

Here

Face both flat hands upward. Then move them in flat circles twice.

"There" in German is "da" (DAH).

There

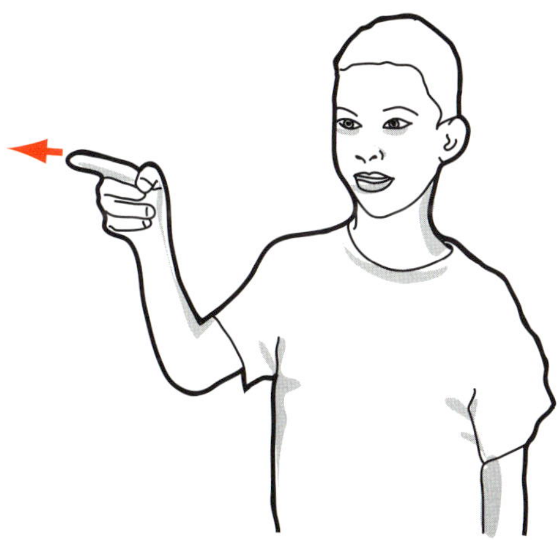

Point away from you.

"Can I?" is sometimes switched with "May I?"

Can I?

Make the "S" sign with both hands. Move both hands downward. Then point to yourself.

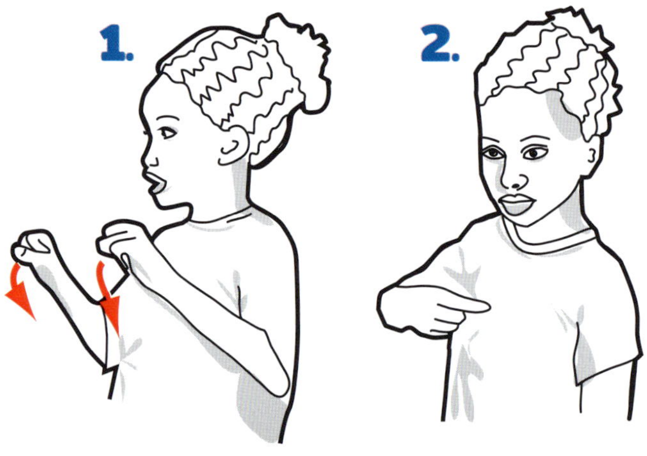

"Will you?" in French is "Voulez-vous?" (VOO-lay VOO).

Will you?

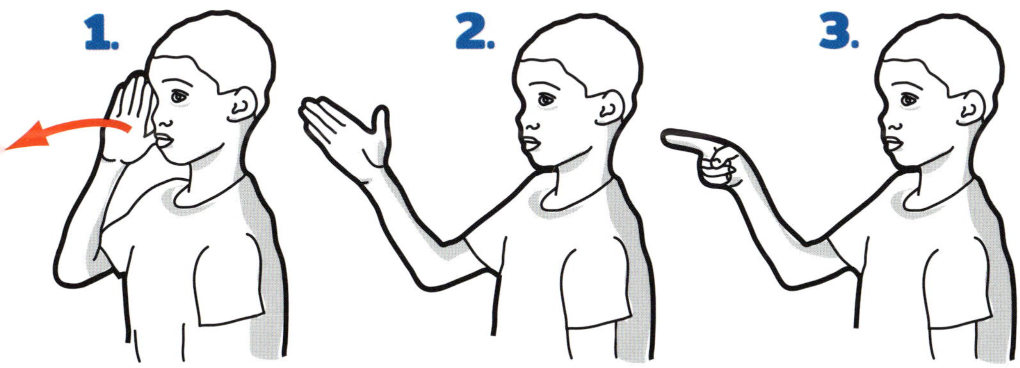

Your flat right hand moves from your face outward. Then point to the person you are speaking to.

A thumbs-up means something is good.

Yes

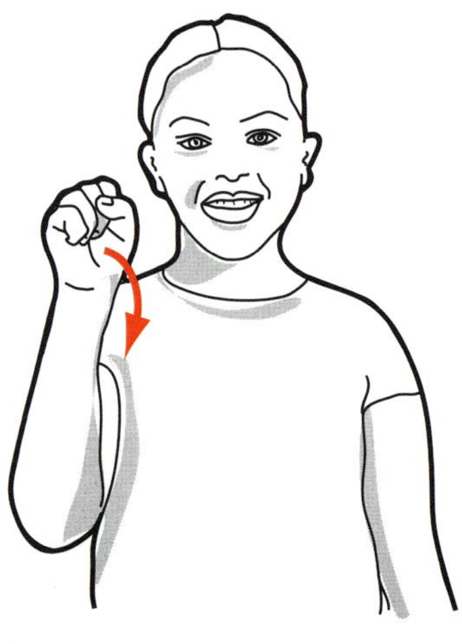

Make the "S" sign with your right hand. Move your wrist downward a few times while nodding your head "yes."

"No" means the same thing in many languages.

No

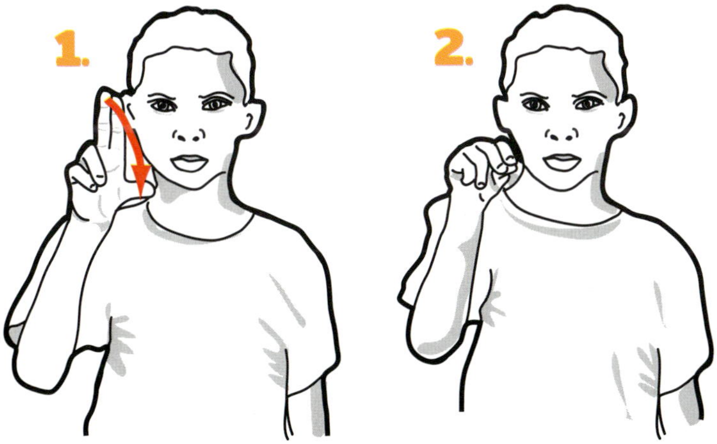

Touch the middle and index fingers of your right hand to your thumb while shaking your head "no."

"How many?" in Japanese is "Ikutsu?" (IH-koot-soo).

How many?

Start with your hands in fists. Then open them both and raise your hands a little.

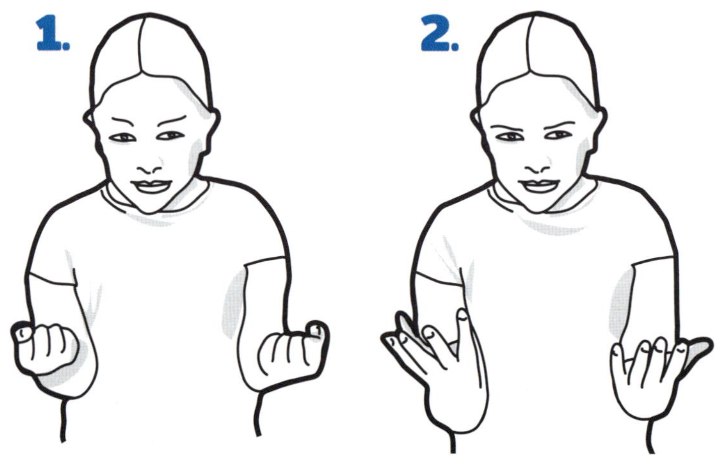

Be sure to check out the alphabet chart on page 23!

All

Spell A-L-L with your fingers.

In ASL, your facial expression can affect the meaning of the sign.

None

Both of your hands make the "O" sign. Move your hands forward quickly while shaking your head "no."

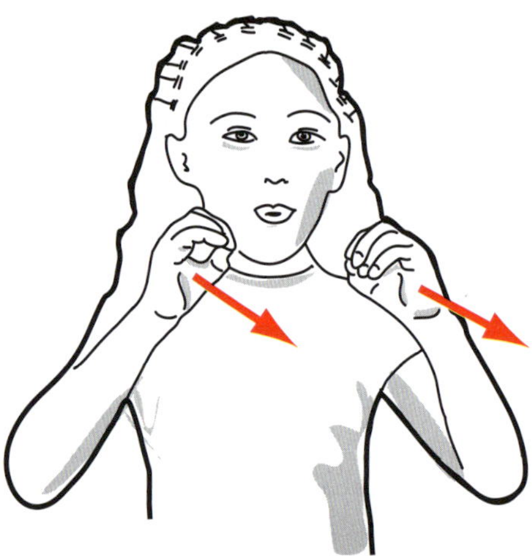

"Why?" in Spanish is "¿Por qué?" (POR KAY).

Why?

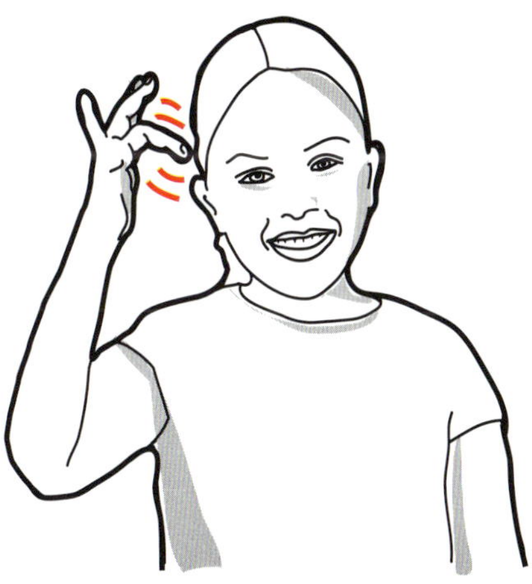

With your hand facing your face, wiggle your right middle finger a few times.

Wonder More

- How much did you know about American Sign Language (ASL) before reading this book? Do you already know some ASL signs? What new signs did you learn?

- Some words or specific names don't have signs. In these cases, you can spell the individual letters of the word, which is called fingerspelling. Look at the alphabet chart on page 23. Can you sign the letters in your name?

- With a partner, pick three signs from this book and practice them together. Are you able to understand each other? Is ASL easier or harder than you thought it would be?

- Do you think it is important to learn ASL? Why or why not? Where can you learn more signs?

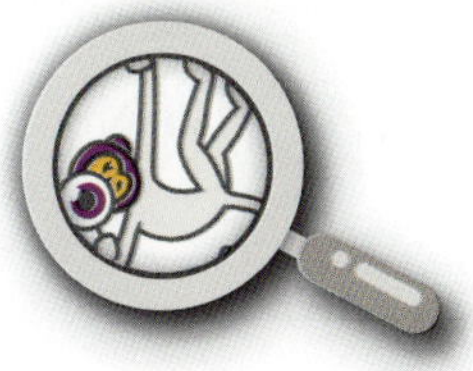

Sign Language Alphabet

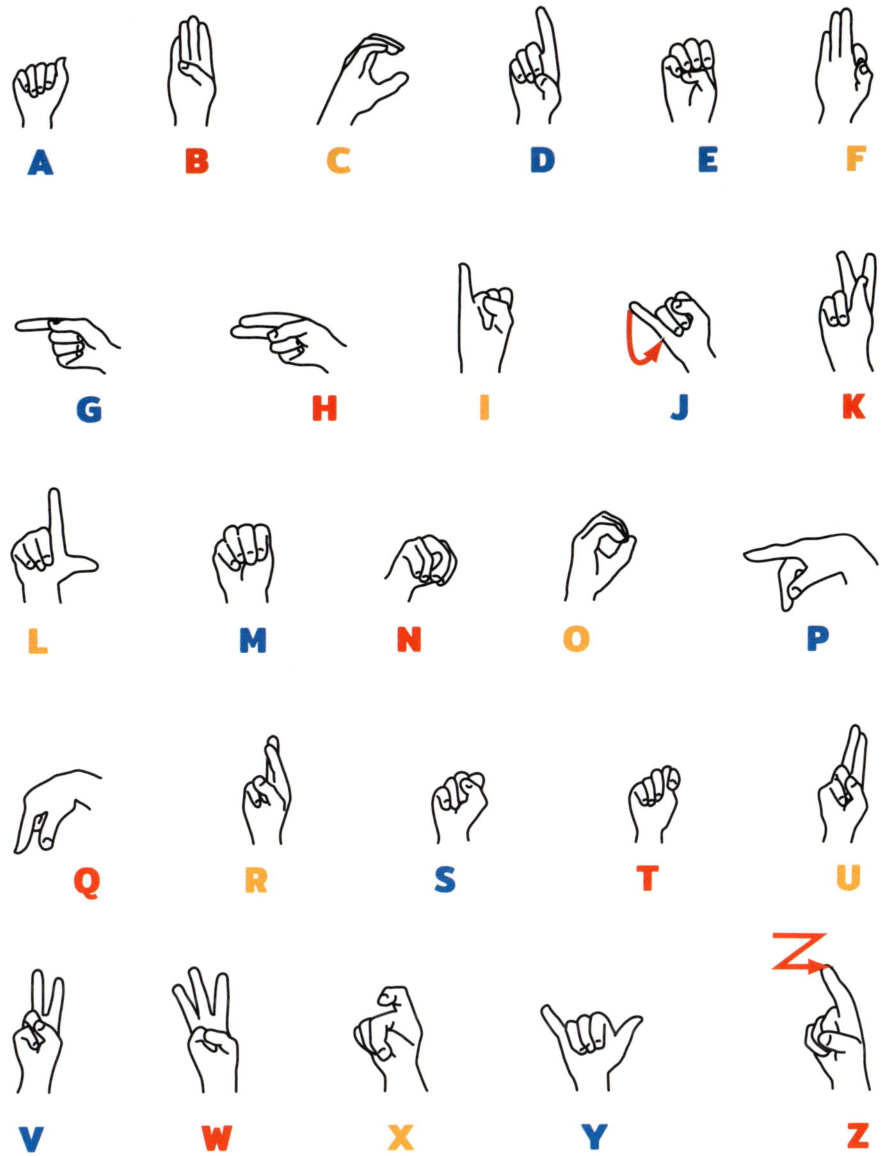

Find Out More

In the Library

Brakenhoff, Kelly, and Caterina Baldi (illustrator). *Sometimes I Like the Quiet* (Duke the Deaf Dog ASL Series). Lincoln, NE: Emerald Prairie Press, 2022.

Gallaudet University Press (editor). *The Gallaudet Children's Dictionary of American Sign Language*. Washington, DC: Gallaudet University Press, 2014.

On the Web

Visit our website for links about American Sign Language:

childsworld.com/links

Note to Parents, Caregivers, Teachers, and Librarians: We routinely verify our web links to make sure they are safe and active sites. So encourage your readers to check them out!

A Special Thank-You!

Thank you to our models from the Program for Children Who are Deaf and Hard of Hearing at the Alexander Graham Bell School in Chicago, Illinois.

Alina's favorite things to do are art, soccer, and swimming. DJ is her brother!

DJ loves playing the harmonica and video games. Alina is his sister!

Dareous likes football. His favorite team is the Detroit Lions. He also likes to play video games.

Jasmine likes writing and math in school. She also loves to swim.

Darionna likes the swings and merry-go-round on the playground. She also loves art.